Our Gross, Awesome World

AWESOME, DISGUSTING, UNUSUAL FACTS ABOUT SPORTS

Eric Braun

BLACK
RABBIT
BOOKS

Hi Jinx is published by Black Rabbit Books
P.O. Box 3263, Mankato, Minnesota, 56002.
www.blackrabbitbooks.com
Copyright © 2019 Black Rabbit Books

Marysa Storm, editor; Michael Sellner, designer;
Catherine Cates, production designer;
Omay Ayres, photo researcher

Library of Congress Cataloging-in-Publication Data
Names: Braun, Eric, 1971- author.
Title: Awesome, disgusting, unusual facts about sports / by Eric Braun.
Description: Mankato, Minnesota : Black Rabbit Books, [2019] |
Series: Hi Jinx. Our Gross, Awesome World | Includes bibliographical
references and index. | Audience: Ages: 9-12. | Audience: Grades: 4 to 6.
Identifiers: LCCN 2017047839 (print) | LCCN 2017050885 (ebook) |
ISBN 9781680726206 (e-book) | ISBN 9781680726145 (library binding) |
ISBN 9781680727562 (paperback)
Subjects: LCSH: Sports–Miscellanea–Juvenile literature. | Sports–Humor.
Classification: LCC GV707 (ebook) | LCC GV707 .A7198 2018 (print) |
DDC 796–dc23
LC record available at https://lccn.loc.gov/2017047839

Printed in the United States. 4/18

Image Credits

Alamy: Deborah Vernon, 16 (middle); PA Images, 14–15; WENN
Ltd, 15; commons.wikimedia.org: Lestalorm, 14; WCBO, 16 (top);
Dreamstime: Andreadonetti, 9 (racket); Liusa, 8 (cows), 21 (cow);
Volykievgenii, 1 (bkgd); Getty: Donald Miralle, 11 (ramp); Jeff Gross,
11 (Way); oregonsportphotos.com: Carole Biskar, 18–19 (woman);
Shutterstock: Aluna1, 7 (bkgd); Andreas H, 16 (bttm); anfisa focusova,
16 (bkgd); Black creater, 7 (golfer); CarpathianPrince, 2–3; Christos
Georghiou, 12 (paper tear); designer_an, 19 (bkgd); Freestyle_stock_
photo, 8 (bkgd); GraphicsRF, 4 (ball, field), 23 (ball); kaisorn, 7
(orange light); Karl Rosencrants, 3 (bkgd), 21 (bkgd); Lima Junior, 8
(cow pattern); Memo Angeles, 9 (sheep); MoreVector, 13 (handshake);
Neale Cousland, 20 (bttm); PA Images, 10 (tennis match); Pasko
Maksim, Back Cover (top), 6 (bttm), 23 (top), 24; Pitju, 21 (page
curl); rodho, 6–7 (flames); Rohit Dhanaji Shinde, 4 (pig), 23 (pig);
Ron Dale, Cover (marker stroke), 1 (marker stroke), 3, 6 (top), 10
(top), 14 (top), 20 (top); Simakova Elena, 10–11 (grass); takoburito,
Cover (football); untitled, 7 (ball); vasosh, 12 (baseball); VectorShots,
7 (ball's expression); wanpatsorn, 8 (football, bkgd); USA Today
Sports Images: Porter Binks, 12 (Abbott) Every effort has been made
to contact copyright holders for material reproduced in this book. Any
omissions will be rectified in subsequent printings if notice is given to
the publisher.

CONTENTS

4

Chapter 1
WELCOME TO THE STRANGE SIDE OF SPORTS

People love to play sports. They're a lot of fun. They can also be pretty gross and weird. Ever heard of a sport played with cheese? How about the importance of animal guts in sports history? Or the handy role of urine in baseball? Well, enough warm-ups! It's time to **kick off.**

Chapter 2

FUNKY FACTS
ABOUT EQUIPMENT

There are many cool facts about sports equipment. For example, golf balls don't have **dimples** just for looks. They decrease **drag**. Less drag means balls fly farther. Most have between 300 and 500 dimples.

In 2008, Speedo introduced a new swimsuit. The suits helped swimmers cut through water more easily. Too easily! Swimmers broke more than 100 world records in just 17 months. Officials banned the suits from competitions.

In 1971, an astronaut hit two golf balls on the moon. They're still there today.

All about Organs

NFL footballs are handmade from cow skin. It takes more than 1,000 cows to make enough footballs for one season.

People made early tennis racket strings from sheep **intestines**. Today, some players still use natural gut strings. But they usually come from cows.

Early soccer balls were made from pig **bladders** covered with leather.

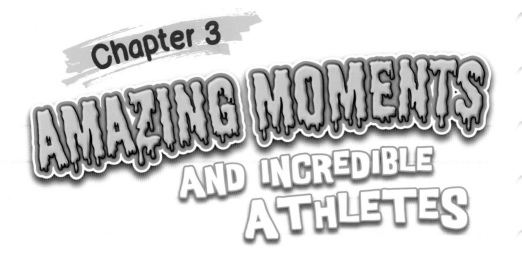

Chapter 3
AMAZING MOMENTS
AND INCREDIBLE ATHLETES

In 1923, a **jockey** couldn't celebrate a race he won. Why? Because he was dead! He had a heart attack during the race. Somehow his body stayed on the horse.

Another amazing moment happened in 2010. A tennis game lasted 11 hours and five minutes. It spanned over three days.

Danny Way holds the record for longest skateboard ramp jump. In 2004, he jumped a distance of 79 feet (24 meters).

Get Ready for Baseball

Jim Abbott was born without a right hand. But that didn't stop him from becoming an amazing pitcher. He pitched left-handed. He taught himself to pull his glove on quickly after throwing. He pitched in the major leagues for 10 years.

Speaking of hands, you should think twice before shaking a big-leaguer's hand. Some baseball players pee on their hands. They believe the pee will help toughen them up.

Abbott pitched a no-hitter in 1993.

Chapter 4
WEIRD, WACKY, OFF-THE-WALL SPORTS

The world is full of strange (and delicious) sports. In the Olney Pancake Race, racers run with skillets full of pancakes. They have to flip those pancakes too!

The sport of cheese rolling is exactly what it sounds like. A wheel of cheese rolls down a hill. Players then chase it. The winner keeps the cheese.

Who knew there were so many food-related sports? Every year, people participate in the World Gravy Wrestling Championships. In it, competitors actually wrestle in a pool of gravy.

chessboxing

toe wrestling

fireball soccer

Unique Sports

Boxing or chess? Why not both? In chessboxing, competitors switch between rounds of chess and boxing.

If you really want to light up the **pitch**, try fireball soccer. Players kick around a flaming coconut soaked in **kerosene**.

Too cool for regular ol' arm wrestling? That's OK. You can toe wrestle. Yup, it's a sport!

On the Water

People don't just race boats. In the Giant Pumpkin **Regatta**, people race carved-out pumpkins.

You could also try milk carton boat racing. In that sport, people race boats made from milk cartons.

Want to win the tin bathtub race? Just cross the finish line in your tin bathtub first. Or make it the farthest before your tub sinks!

Chapter 5
GET IN ON THE HI JINX

There are many amazing sports moments yet to happen. Many people call Serena Williams one of history's greatest tennis players. The company IBM is looking for the next Williams. It gathers **statistics** on pro tennis players. It examines young players with similar strengths. Will they become the next big stars?

Take It One Step More

1. Do you think statistics and technology make sports more or less fun? Why?

2. Sports have changed a lot over the years. What changes do you think will happen in the future?

3. If you could invent a new sport, what would it be?

GLOSSARY

bladder (BLAD-er)—an organ in the body that holds urine after it passes through the kidneys and before it leaves the body

dimple (DIM-puhl)—a small area on the surface that curves in

drag (DRAYG)—something that makes action or progress slower or more difficult

intestine (en-TE-sten)—the part of the digestive system where most food is digested; it is a long tube made up of the small intestine and the large intestine.

jockey (JOK-ee)—someone who rides horses in races

kerosene (KER-uh-seen)—a type of oil that is burned as fuel

pitch (PICH)—a soccer field

regatta (ri-GAT-uh)—a race or series of races between boats

statistic (stuh-TIS-tik)—a number that represents a piece of information

BOOKS

Braun, Eric. *Incredible Sports Trivia: Fun Facts and Quizzes.* Trivia Time! Minneapolis: Lerner Publications, 2018.

Mason, Tyler. *Football Trivia.* Sports Trivia. Minneapolis: SportsZone, an imprint of Abdo Publishing, 2016.

Weird but True Sports: 300 Wacky Facts about Awesome Athletics. Washington, D.C.: National Geographic, 2016.

WEBSITES

Interesting Sports Science Facts
www.sciencekids.co.nz/sciencefacts/ sportsscience.html

SI Kids: Sports News for Kids, Kids Games and More
www.sikids.com

Sports Facts for Kids
www.softschools.com/ facts/sports/

INDEX